A BETTER WAY

In life there are no opposites just equals – same
In life we fear but know not what we fear
There is a reason why I chose this picture but that reasoning is for me alone.

There is a better way in life but that better we cannot find because we've been conditioned to think one way. Hence we are conditioned to think opposites attract. Opposites do not attract because in all the goodness I've seen, good is always trying to escape from evil. Want nothing to do with evil hence evil pulls not attract. Evil pulls you towards it.

Evil controls
Dominate
Kill

Hence the Ying and Yang to many are opposites but in true truth they are the same. They have no difference and distinction but to man they are distinct different. Good and evil. Good versus evil. If you know not the Ying and Yang you cannot know life because life is simple but it is not what you think. There is life and death but in truth there is only life. Water is life hence water is the beginning and end of life. But is there truly an end when it comes to life. I say not hence water cleans, purify, expand – grow. Easy to comprehend for me but hard for you.

As beautiful and simple as the fish, humanity cannot comprehend it nor can they grasp the truth of it.

For those who know, know this symbol to be life the truth of Good God and his life because life is represented by the number 13. 13 months hath we (man). 13 months was given to live but that one day the 365th day belongs to Good God and the goodness that you do on this day for him.

MICHELLE JEAN

A better day comes because the commentary above is abstract, wrong to some of you.

13 is the fear of man
In the year 13 the devil would give his power to a human – man.

This has been done but yet humanity do not know this but I did tell them this in 2013.

The transfer took place and shortly woe be unto man.

A better day comes

Yes a new slavery will be born – begin
Babylon's System has come to earth

Many will be left homeless and penniless, but that is the choice humanity made.

We followed evil to our graves
We allowed sin to deceive us

A new Babylonian order will take fold
This is their new world order of domination and control.

This must be hence the devil has won for the many – billions of humans. But for the chosen few we must now leave. We must Exodus and ride out the waves – tidal waves and storms of hell that will now dominate and control earth.

Slavery is here and there will be no redemption for many.

Redemption Songs we will no longer have

Redemption stories will no longer be told

Redemption draws nigh – near for some but no redemption will be had for billions. They have the tattoos of death already and they too must die. Hell is now on earth because Satan is pissed at his people and now he must take them and leave earth to her own – her good and true people.

Death now comes hence soon the wicked and evil – those that gave themselves over to death must walk and go into the valleys of the dead.

There will be no more rising sun for them. Just a blinding light that takes away their sight.

They will go too and fro and nothing they do will make them find their way – save them.

Michelle Jean

It will be a better day and way for the true but hell for the wicked and evil.

If you were to upload Jah Cure's Prison Walls you will see the hell that many will face because hell is a prison – a jailhouse that no one can escape. The only difference with hell's prison is that it is more severe.

You will be held in a containment unit surrounded by fire and your spirit will burn.

You will pray and cry for rescue but no rescue will come.

No one will save you.

Your spirit must burn until your time comes for your spirit to die.

No visitor will you have
No food will you have
No water will you have to drink

You have to go through it worse than anything you've ever known.

You will pray and cry out that you will be a better person just like in the song.

You will say I will not do it again

You will cry for your freedom and none will be given.

You will cry for sunlight, a chance to redeem yourself but you will get no redemption.

Your livity will be that of hell

There are no second or third chances

Hell is not a game and no matter what you say or do you will burn.

That containment unit is yours alone in that pit of hell.

The demons of hell will do unto you worse than you did on earth. You are in their domain and there are no wages of sin in their world. This is their world – domain and Good God has nothing to do with them or this world. Good God cannot interfere with them because you gave yourself over to them and you are truly going to pay and pay dearly.

You will cry to be set freed, so truly listen to this song because for many, you have no freedom and will get none.

Michelle Jean

I've told you Black People are in prison in hell right now. I opened the door in my dream and no one took the chance to escape, so they were left in hell.

They sat there in hell because they were faithful to death – hell. You as Blacks know this in the living so take your chance and escape the clutches of death – hells fire.

You have your escape take it BECAUSE NO MORE WILL COME AND SAVE YOU – RESCUE YOU AGAIN. This is your final chance so take it.

Start living truthfully. You have the opportunity now so take it. You will not get another chance to do so. So truly live and stop the wrongs – sins that you are doing.

THE WAGES OF SIN IS DEATH BUT TRUTH IS EVERLASTING LIFE. So if you know truth is everlasting life, then live by your truths – the truth of Good God and stop sinning.

Good God is the better way so choose the better way for you and your family as well as your good friends.

Like I've told Good God. If I could give him all that is good and true I would but I cannot. I too have sinned. I live for truth and run from all evil hence I depend on him Good God.

Yes I have my moments when I lash out at him and humanity. I do not cuss and lash out because I hate. I lash out and curse my own for them to smarten up and see that hell is not a bed of roses. My people need to stop sitting on their asses and get up. Do for self and save self. Do not wait until the last minute when it's too late and sey yu a run fi ketch Good God – his ark. You will be too late. You will not catch the ark of Good God.

Do not be like the neglectful people in Noah's time in your book of sin because Noah's time is now. The flood comes. Many lands will be left barren – dry and many will lose it all to war and floods. You do not want to get caught up in this hell hole of a mess shortly. So truly know your goodness and what you are doing.

I truly need you to live for you.

I truly, infinitely truly do not want to see any of you go to hell.

I truly don't want to see deaths children go to hell and burn but it's the choice they made. They do not want to save themselves – self.

Like I've said time and time again. _Good God locks no one out of his kingdom we are the ones to lock ourselves out._

Evil's children do not have to die. They too can be saved but they have to walk away from evil on their own.

The fighting and hatred have to stop.
Must stop.

The murder and rape have to stop.
Must stop.

The destruction have to stop.
Must stop.

The blame game must stop.

A person that is good and true cannot truly hate you. We can however hate the wickedness and evils that you do.

This is why I petition Good God to end it. End this madness – war between North and South. It must stop because lives are being taken and it's not right nor is it fair to humans. _Everyone has a right to life – good life and it is not right for sin to maliciously take our life from us. Come on now._

Hell is real

The fires of hell is real and no one should want to go there.

Listen to this man, Jah Cure when he said, **prison is not a bed of rose.** We know prison is not a bed of rose because you are locked away from society.

So if prison is not a bed of rose, why want to go there?

Why sin to go to hell?

You have no freedom

You have no hope because you've become hopeless.

You have no escape because there is absolutely no escaping hell.

You are trapped – caged like an animal in this 4 x 4 or 6 x 6 square wall. *In hell it's a oval type container surrounded by fire – spiritual fire not earthly fire.*

You cannot do certain things. In hell you cannot do anything.

You have no freedom to walk

A BETTER WAY

You have no freedom to talk

You have no freedom to go see your family

You have no freedom to make love to your mate

You cannot kiss your children if you have any

You cannot hug your children if you need a hug

You cannot see your children grow

You cannot see them grow up to be the good person you need them to be

You can't drink a beer or a shot of rum with your friends

You cannot run a boat of dumpling and chicken back, fish, itals with your friends

You cannot go see your favorite artist perform

You cannot pick a mango off di mango tree

You cannot hail up your friend if you want to

You will lose your friends and family

You will lose it all because after your prison time is done on earth, you are going to go to hell and face fire harsher than the fires of earth.

When your family and friends are in Good God's kingdom depending on if your family and friends were good, you will be in hell burning. This is why some Black Mother's pray and beg Good God for the goodness of their children on earth. Listen to Black Mother Pray by Tarrus Riley. This is reality for the true mother's of earth that truly love their children. We pray hard and sometimes the tears come when we pray because I am a testament of this. We are to truly love our children and teach them right. If you are wicked and evil and has been sentenced to death, you are going to cry out for a saving grace and will get none. No one is going to save you because there is no saving grace for you. No one is permitted to save you in hell. <u>*YOU ARE HOME, HENCE YOU GAVE YOUR SOUL – SPIRIT TO DEATH ON EARTH.*</u> Death gave you a home – his home and in this home you will stay until your eventual death. When your family and friends (depending on goodness) are drinking the pure and good waters of Good God's abode and eating the good foods of him Good God, you will be in hell burning and suffering because of the wrongs you did on earth.

Yes many have and has faced hell on earth but your struggles on earth is not hell. And trust me you don't want to go to hell.

Fiya hot but no fiya no hot lacka hell fiya.

Di sun wey yu look an si, no hot lacka hell fiya.

This fire, hell's fire was specifically made and designed by humans of earth – your sins. We are the ones that created hell hence unto hell many must go to die.

No one can blame hell on Good God because it was not Good God that sinned we were and still are the ones to sin not him. *(And yes, I've blamed him Good God for hell. But hell he did not create. Death and hell comes about due to our sins – our vile and wicked ways.)*

We are the ones to walk away from him Good God without thinking of the consequences.

We talk about vileness without thinking about self. W are the vile ones because we sin.

We hate each other and others

We design chemicals and weapons to kill

We are the ones to lie – accept the lies of sin.

A BETTER WAY

We are the ones to have children we cannot afford hence we deal in slavery – human trafficking as it is known today.

We are the ones to sacrifice self, children, others in humanity to death for a place in hell without knowing that in all the wickedness that you do, sacrificing others, you are going to go to hell and burn as well.

Evil cannot promise you a good place in hell because there are no good places in hell.

Evil cannot say he or she is going to give you air conditionings in hell because there are no air conditioners in hell.

Evil cannot tell you there are many mansions in his father's house because the mansions in his father's house are the pits of fire that is going to contain your spirit in hell. This fire is going to burn you. So tell me how can pits of fire be mansions when they are hell?

How can these pits be mansions when there are no beds?

No PSP
No cell phones
No televisions

A BETTER WAY

No water
No food
No bathroom to bathe

No restaurants
No fast food joints
No vacation homes – property
No jetliners and fast cars
No private jets

There are no sports teams in hell. You will be the sport of death to do whatever he feels like doing with.

How can these pits be mansions, when you will not see anyone? Not even your wife and kids.

You will not be able to see your girlfriend because you are alone in this pit. You will however see your demons which are your sins and these demons can do whatever they want to do with you because pain they know. **_DEMONS LIVE FOR HURT AND PAIN, THIS I INFINITELY AND INDEFINITELY KNOW._** No pain that is inflicted on you on earth compares to the pain and suffering these demons of hell will do to you.

Satan cannot save you. So if you think all is going to be fine on earth because Satan transferred his power to a man, truly think again.

Satan does not like to lose and he did lose in the spiritual realm. So truly woe be unto you his people because he gave his power to him to inflict pain and he must do what Satan says. **_HE MUST ENSLAVE AND MAKE YOU THE PRISONERS OF DEATH. THAT IS THE LAW. Thus saith the Lord thy God meaning it is so._**

Wow truly woe be unto many of you.

Demons know how to inflict pain and you will be in pain until your sentence is up and you die indefinitely forever ever.

No chance will you have to live again.

Michelle Jean

Some of you are saying. if I can face it in the prisons of earth, I can face it and make it in the prisons of hell. And to all that is saying this. Truly good luck because I infinitely truly know otherwise.

<u>Hell's prison does not make you stronger it makes you dead because you are dying a slow and painful death.</u>

Like I've said, no one makes it out of hell.

<u>NO ONE HAS EVER ESCAPED DEATH BECAUSE NO ONE CAN ESCAPE DEATH.</u>

You signed an unbreakable contract with death and this is the contract death has. Not even Good God himself can interfere and break this contract. Hence I tell you what belongs to death is his. You chose death not life so you must go to death and die.

<u>AND NO YOU CANNOT SUE DEATH BECAUSE THERE ARE NO COURTS OF LAW IN HELL.</u>

Once your flesh hits the grave your sins are told to you. You are told how much time you have to spend in hells fire before you eventually die.

So if you are a politician that say you govern the people of your land and you have say 163

A BETTER WAY

million people in your land. Say that 163 million people have and has committed let's say 10 million sins each. **And don't say a man cannot commit 10 million sins in his lifetime because he can. You do not know the weight and or value of that sin.**

Oh man I did not talk about the value of a sin. Well I cannot talk about it because I truly do not know the weight and or value for each sin. I know some sins are automatic death and I've told you them.

So multiply 163 million by 10 million sins plus whatever time death tacks on for good measure. And don't forget in your multiplication to multiply that figure by 24000 years before you tack on the good measure of death. On top of that add your sins and the sins of your wife and child to that total and you will get the time you will spend in hell's fire before you die.

And death does not have to go by spiritual time. Your time in hell can be earthly time that is slowed down.

Don't go there with but you said time is constant.

Yes time is constant and can never change for humanity – humans. You are dealing with a

18

different time and death's time is not human's time.

Death's time is not Good God's time.

Death's time is death's time.

Death is the owner and keeper of his time because his time can vary. Hence death mask death and he can mask his time.

But, but, but.

There are no buts about this. This is your reality.

This is the reality of man – humanity because like I said, no one chose life, you chose death.

<u>You listened to someone tell you, death is a good thing and you can become a god and or live good and free. You did not realize that person sacrificed you to death. You were his or her sacrifice and he or she did sacrifice you without you even knowing it. This is why I warn my children on their friends and the music they listen to. Certain places they know not to go already. I just have to warn them about the different lands.</u>

A BETTER WAY

You know it's amazing how I tell people – family members that Jamaica has been deemed unclean and they are not hearing me. They're not listening to me. They want to go to Jamaica. **_As ole people sey, wha sweet nanny goat a go run dem belly. Mi warn and who no hear muss feel._** So if you think what I say is a lie go ahead and go to Jamaica. I know the tattooed eye you will see and truly woe be unto you in the end. **_Because if your name was in the book of life already and you defy the words of Good God and go into Jamaica, your name will infinitely and indefinitely no longer be in the book of life, it will be in the book of death._**

From the time yu go book di ticket consider yourself dead – a part of the dead.

Now let me ask you this. If death is a god and he owns hell and all that is in hell how are you going to be a god?

You have to bow down to death and kiss his ass if he tells you to, so how are you a god or going to become a god?

If death owns your spirit and soul how can you be a god?

Are you not the slave and bitch of death?

Well I can overthrow death you are saying.

And I'm telling you right now death is smiling and shaking his head and calling you a fool.

<u>**If Satan himself cannot overthrow death, how the hell do you think you can overthrow death?**</u>

Absolutely no one can overthrow death. Not even Good God himself because Good God does not deal in death he deals in life.

Whatever is given to death he death takes. He does not give back and I've told you this.

But you opened the door of hell for your people and family to take in your dream?

You did not open the door for the white race?

<u>**What belongs to death belongs to death. The white race belongs to death because they were the ones to be cursed hence I could not save those that were in hell. They were separated from the Black Race.**</u>

<u>**I can only save my own which are Blacks. Those who fall under the banner of black.**</u>

A BETTER WAY

But you said some whites are black?

So if you know this why are we having this conversation?

Are there not White Jamaicans? Dem sey dem white but dem blacka dan mi an yu. They fall under the banner of black. You cannot touch them because they are well protected.

Now go back to the beginning of the book

What do you see?

The Ying and Yang you've answered.

Good, now look at the colours.

Do you not have black in white and white in black?

Yes you are saying or have answered.

Now you know life. True life.

Now I ask. What the hell we are doing when we fight amongst each other?

Are we not taking away from life?

Are we not killing life?

But it's not that simple as you make it out to be.

It is that simple. We as humans make it hard because we all think we are better than each other.

No one is better than any. And the money you accumulate and make does not make you better than the next man. We all die the same in the end if we are evil and many of us are evil.

Michelle Jean

Don't even go there about the marriage thing.

Go back to the Ying and Yang because it is okay.

<u>There are no buts because no one can dilute the spirit, you can only kill it.</u>

If your preference is White it's your preference.

If your preference is Black it is your preference.

Oh lord here comes the evil ones that are saying I am an hypocrite for the way I write. Too bad kiss my ass because I make no distinction between Good God's children. I will however make the distinction between evil's wicked children and what they do to Life.

I have to write certain ways due to the content of the spirit. I too have to get Africa – Africans to wake up. **<u>I have to get the black race to wake up and truly walk away from death BECAUSE DEATH BROUGHT COLOUR INTO THIS.</u>**

<u>DEATH DID NOT TELL YOU THERE IS A BLACK DEATH AND A WHITE DEATH. BLACK DEATH TAKES THE FLESH. MEANING RELEASE THE SPIRIT FROM ITS FLESHY PRISION.</u>

WHITE DEATH IS FINAL DEATH FOR ALL WHO ARE EVIL. THE EVIL AND OR DEMON THAT POSSES YOU, WHITE DEATH IS THE ONE TO SEPARATE AND KILL IT NOT BLACK DEATH. HENCE WHEN EVIL DIES, EVIL DIES AS WHITE (A WHITE PERSON) DRESSED IN WHITE.

SO AS BLACK DEATH SEPARATES SPIRIT FROM FLESH, WHITE DEATH SEPARATES EVIL FROM YOUR SPIRIT AND KILL IT.

Your sins you are accountable for hence the separation all around. So if I did not clarify this in my other books you now have full clarification and the full truth.

Why should I hate you based on the colour of your skin?

Did the colour of your skin say Michelle I hate your back ass because it's just plain out black and ugly and I don't like it?

Did my skin colour say I hate your white ass because it's just plain out ugly, raw and uncooked?

No your skin did not tell me this nor did my skin tell you this. So why the bleep should I hate you based on colour of skin.

Did the colour of your skin make weapons of mass destruction to annihilate humanity especially black people?

Did the colour of your skin and my skin say I can get you into Good God's kingdom? Or was it you the person that said these things and did these things?

Well I don't like your skin colour. And I say to you it's not your skin that's telling me it does not like my skin colour it's you.

Your spirit has and have found fault in me – all that is around me not your skin.

HENCE IT'S NOT YOUR SKIN THAT BURNS IN HELL, IT'S YOUR SPIRIT.

Michelle Jean

A BETTER WAY

Yes it's a better way and I am looking forward to a better day and a better way of life.

I am looking forward to truth, the rising of a new sun and moon of goodness and truth.

Life isn't about death it's about life
The truth of life – your life

A New World Order begins and this world order will not be pretty for some.

The exodus of good from evil lands must begin
Death must walk and take his own

Dreams are weird this morning hence I will not include them in this book because I broadcast it on twitter.

The reign of evil – terror is here.
The time has come for humanity to pay and pay dearly for their wicked and sinful deeds.

Hence the New World Order of Sin is here. The harvest comes and truly woe be unto man – humanity.

Michelle Jean

If I could Good God I would but I cannot

Humanity is truly going to need you but what's done is done.

All that we did in the dark must come to the light.

The new king of Babylon must stand and rule his people because they are his.

I know the slavery that is to come because he – Death wants slavery for all who follow him.

He death must have slavery because the vileness of man has gone on for far too long. All we did, we did sin vile and wicked and truly woe be unto man when death is done in the living and spirit.

Death cannot be controlled.

He must take what's his and bring your spirit to the grave for sentence because the grave is the Court of Justice for all that is wicked and evil.

Evil's fate is read here and it is here (in the grave) that you will find out where you go.

Many will not escape the fate of death because in all that we do to sin we forgot sins pay.

Death's pay!!!

Michelle Jean

A BETTER WAY

It's February 02, 2014 and I cannot end this book because I so do not know what to write anymore.

I've been listening to Nesian Nine and Pieter T and I am going to endorse them because it's a new year and a better way.

Yes it's a better way and I so need to find me a man from the South Pacific.

Damn the men are fine and hot, hot, hot.

Nice and fat. Just the way I like them.

Wow, koodles to Hawaiian, Samoan and New Zealand man. Gorgeous, very gorgeous.

Yes people I am crazy but hey that's me.

So to the sisters that are looking for someone different, just look to the South Pacific because you can so look.

Dem man dey fat and nice. A true teddy bear dem. For real because truss mi di brothers can sing. And I know Nesian Nine and Pieter T is not from the South Pacific but the facial features are the same. To me people, so please don't come with the hatred here. Or the No, we are different and all that jazz. In my book if I say you are, you are and that's a good thing.

I just discovered the song Seasons by Nesian Nine featuring Pieter T and I am so in love.

Dexton Ennis, Shaggy, Ne-Yo, Morgan Heritage, VP Records, Sony, take a listen at how music is done because the JT's of your music catalogues are crap in my book compared to good music and singing like this. Pieter T you do it for me. Nesian Nine keep up the good work because your voice is awesome.

Season got me. Move over Tarrus Riley and TGT because you truly have some amazing competition.

Pieter T it would be you on this day baby because you are simply amazing. This colab with Nesian is Boom. Brap, Brap. Damn you and Nesian Nine a gwaane.

Amazing, Amazing. I truly love this song. Tarrus, I am the radio station now and I've added Nesian and Pieter T to my playlist along with TGT.

Damn you no longer have the monopoly in my world. So you had better come up with some more good music.

Nesian and Pieter T you got me.

Yu hot.

Cover up for me though Pieter because I so don't like your tattoos. No, you tainted your beautiful body – skin with dem tats. So for me in your videos do not let me see your tats. It takes away from your beauty – beauty of skin.

Truly love your music. Listen baby it's the New Year and I am raving about you and Nesian Nine's Seasons.

<u>Yes I know you have Right Here and Rumors but baby the seasons will do just fine because wow.</u>

Come on Nesian Nine keep me warm.

It's winter and I need warmth. Nesian anytime you want to do a collaboration with TGT just let me know so that I can fall – utterly fall out of my chair and say yeah baby I'm in heaven.

Keep music like Seasons coming because I'm hooked.

Pieter T yeah. Just keep your love for me the same over the years and hold the music down for me and never leave me.

Yes I need your love for all seasons especially in the autumn and winter. Trust me I will keep it pushing so we can argue as long as you keep the bed warm so we can do our thing.

Laugh because I am one crazy writer. Your music do this to me bring out the crazy in me and that's a good thing.

Clooney, George that is. Take a walk on the black side so that a sister can rock your world to great music like this.

And everyone make New Zealand and Samoa a part of your vacation package because for the scenery looks magnificent and untainted. Man I so want to go to New Zealand and spend some time there. The fondness of the heart people.

Michelle Jean

A BETTER WAY

People if you truly love good music as I do, you have to get buck wild and push it.

Like I've said, my musical taste is not conditioned by anyone or anything.

My children are the same way.

In my home the listening field are as follows.

Hard – Acid Rock
Rap
Dancehall – hardcore
K Pop and Nigerian Pop

Reggae
Soul – RNB

I can't box my children in. I just tell them not to get absorbed into the artists that glorify evil – the devil. I tell them I do not like them to listen to their music but the choice is up to them.

I have no problem with certain music. When you glorify evil then I have a problem with it. And no I cannot listen to hard rock – acid rock. Wow don't let me get into this type of music because Acid rock is not music to me. It kills the ear drums. If you like it like one of my child, you are truly brave and koodles to you.

Michelle Jean

Hey shout out to Black Adonis who is doing his thing.

Check out his quotes on twitter.

Got to support my brother from another mother. Hence I am looking forward to getting a copy of his book when it comes out. So Black Adonis make your book a reality so I can get a copy and quote you.

Da Professor I don't know why you are on my mind hence shout out to you yet again. Keep doing your thing.

Marcus Peters, I know you have a good voice so take note from Pieter T and Nesian – music Seasons. Listen to the voice.

Listen to TGT and do your thing because good music can never die. It's universal and good music keep life and this universe going.

Think vibrations.

Sound vibrates hence vibration affect your spirit. Causes you to move – vibrate.

The reason why I am talking about vibrations is because I saw a video of Jah Cure's live in Negril – Turtleman TV January 2014. The guy is damned good live. He has a voice but that's not what got to me. What got to me was that the people were not really dancing – moving.

You are at a concert and if you have room to dance move your damned feet and dance.

Dance and stop being a stiff dick that need a release. Enjoy the music as well as yourself. I don't care if he's not your artist, it does not stop you from moving to good music.

Trust me if and when I go to a live concert. I will be dancing because I am going to take my niece with me and I'll be dancing with her and grooving to the groove. Jamaican people truly learn to enjoy yourself because the music does not define you or your personality. Stop being boxed in. The universe and world is not boxed in so why are you?

Good music is life so truly enjoy life.

I came to enjoy myself and get my money's worth come on now and I will not be stiff trust me.

I know the live music will not sound like the record but hell the beat must be like the record.

No. I cannot comprehend nor can I understand or overstand why anyone would pay so much money to stand there and watch an artist perform. Move the body and enjoy.

No it come eene like when mi watch CVM news on the internet. No take a look at the Jamaican news. Di reporter dem dead lacka dem jus a come outta grave yard or dem a vampire anna just come out fi di night an dey a look food.

No people dem boring. Truss mi listening to dem make yu feel suicidal to rass.

Di set boring, the delivery of the news boring. A di dead dem work for.

To the owners of CVM Jamaica revamp your damned sets. Get the reporters out of the damned office and mek dem deliver di news pon di streets sometimes.

Truss mi, mi love courts and I truly cannot tell you why. Courts hold a beautiful spot in my heart.

Make arrangements to do the news in a courts living room or something. I know the life in Jamaica is disheartening but it does not mean you are to give us boring people to add to our misery. Come on now.

A BETTER WAY

No, di owna dem wey own CVM Jamaica damn boring maybe that's why they hire boring reporters.

And dress di oman dem properly for God's sake. Laade have mercy wey dem get dem clothes. No, anno Salvation Army because Salvation Army sell used clothing. No a di ugly donation box dem get dem clothes from.

No a long time mi waane get mad pan CVM and this is not the right book for it I know but mi run out of things fi sey das why wi a go dis route.

But for real someone need to do something with the afternoon reporter. Choose colour that suits your color.

Red lipstick no fit black people. Get proper makeup because unnu look like unnu a bleach. No, the afternoon female reporter needs a complete overhaul.

News people are not to look shabby. Dress comfortable. If you don't need a jacket, lose it!!

Get comfortable with the job and on the job.

Maybe it's the pay, the low paying job?

A BETTER WAY

No, I don't think so because the warmth of the island should be enough to put a smile on anyone's face.

Also get someone else to do Inspire Jamaica. Du mi a beg yu. Please get someone else to do Inspire Jamaica. I don't know who but get someone more real and down to earth.

Inspire Jamaica should not be a job it should be something you truly love to do. I should want to watch this program and tell people others about it but the show lacks something for me.

Yes I have a lot to say but I'm just saying. Stop with the boring crap.

Entertainment report I can hardly find on the internet.

Denise Hunt a miss you girl.

Yu skinny yes but you had spunk. A miss yu.

Denise Hunt where are you. CVM truly needs you. Go du di news no.

Deniseeeeeeeeeeeee where can I find you.

No mi naa comment bout di man dem because dem just put mi to sleep.

Dem no bad but mi no waane listen to dem. Boring. Yes I have to sit through a boring set and boring voices to go with it.

Revamp the set. Make the reporters stand up as if they are interacting with their audience.

And no truly do not look at me because I am not a set designer.

Oh Garfield or however you pronounce your name, please stop for me. It's 2014 and I cannot find your show on the internet. Hence someone did us a favour and took you off air. You don't have swag and the likkle wey yu sey yu have is not happening.

Tacky will always be tacky hence I am so glad you're gone.

Truss mi, if Jamaica was not so dirty – unclean, I would bring flavour to your TV.

Just kidding because I am not an exciting person. I am looking for excitement myself hence I truly don't seek boredom.

Michelle Jean

A BETTER WAY

Before mi go mi glad fi di likkle bit wey mi si pan Turtleman TV.

Turtleman TV wow because a Jamaica dat. So send me the link for you. You are truly Jamaica because if you look at the picture of Jamaica, you see two turtles that are joined not separated. Hence the turtle go from land to sea and from sea to land. Bless up.

Now mi a listen to some man wey a chat.

Jamaican man love chat bout dem no eat unda sheet eeene. Laade if I was a hotel and motel room, bed and wall that could chat. Truss mi, mi woulda talk. Mi no love secret because what's done in the dark must come to light.

All some oman bought dem naa bow and dem tongue like anaconda, rackla, sugar cane, rod of iron, broom stick and you name it inna hairy motel.

Truss mi, the receiver no need a man because di tongue a do di job betta dan di man to regile. Mi naa chat did name of the person but some a dem dancehall oman dey fi go si dung because dem secret dung buss in the spiritual realm already.

A BETTER WAY

Some a dem man wey a chat bout dem no bow fi go si dung because like I said, if I was a hotel and motel room, bed and wall mi woulda chat.

Truss mi people, di tabloids dem would have nothing on me because mi woulda chat long before it happen. Wait mi do dat aready. Scrap that mi a tabloid, hence these books.

Mek mi tell yu something. Fi mi mouth no ha kina when it comes to chat wey mi si. Jamaica if mi open fi mi mouth pon some a unnu artist and people dem, nuff a unnu cry. Mi do dat aready fi some so scrap this too.

So to the reggae and dancehall artists' wey a lick out bout bow cats anna sey unnu no bow stop. Unnu no ha secret because mi si dem.

MOSE A UNNU NO BOW A YAADE BUT WHEN UNNU GO ABROAD HOTEL AND MOTEL ROOM A LAUGH AN A CHAT.

Unnu bow hence unnu dance abroad in a different way.

Your doings are not concealed so truly stop.

Stop being a hypocrite because some a unnu name MR. DO IT RIGHT under sheet.

A BETTER WAY

Some a unnu gi curly feet das why other nations love unnu so. Unnu nyam anna lie. Some a unnu love fi smell hence unnu natural high.

Some a unnu bout Rasta Man no do dem things dey, but yet Rasta Man do dem things dey.

Some a unnu sey unnu no nyam pork but behind closed doors the pork is on the table, unnu nyam pork.

Stop sey a lie because the majority of you do not read the labels of packaging's. A lot of food say all beef but when you read the label, pork is listed as one of the ingredients.

We say we eat chicken but yet beside the chicken pork dey beside it. Hence the lack of respect when it comes to certain rights – your fundamental clean rights.

Yes some of you maybe clean but it does not mean your surroundings are clean. So truly do not say you don't when you do.

Michelle Jean

OTHER BOOKS BY MICHELLE JEAN

Blackman Redemption – The Fall of Michelle Jean
Blackman Redemption – After the Fall Apology
Blackman Redemption – World Cry – Christine Lewis
Blackman Redemption
Blackman Redemption – The Rise and Fall of Jamaica
Blackman Redemption – The War of Israel
Blackman Redemption – The Way I Speak to God
Blackman Redemption – A Little Talk With Man
Blackman Redemption – The Den of Thieves
Blackman Redemption – The Death of Jamaica
Blackman Redemption – Happy Mother's Day
Blackman Redemption – The Death of Faith
Blackman Redemption – The War of Religion
Blackman Redemption – The Death of Russia
Blackman Redemption – The Truth
Blackman Redemption – Spiritual War

The New Book of Life
The New Book of Life – A Cry For The Children
The New Book of Life – Judgement
The New Book of Life – Love Bound
The New Book of Life - Me

Just One of Those Days
Book Two – Just One of Those Days
Just One of Those Days – Book Three The Way I Feel
Just One of Those Days – Book Four

The Days I Am Weak
Crazy Thoughts – My Book of Sin
Broken

A BETTER WAY

Ode to Mr. Dean Fraser

A Little Little Talk
A Little Little Talk – Book Two

Prayers
My Collective
A Little Talk/A Time For Fun and Play
Simple Poems
Behind The Scars
Songs of Praise And Love

Love Bound
Love Bound – Book Two

Dedication Unto My Kids
More Talk
Saving America From A Woman's Perspective
My Collective the Other Side of Me
My Collective the Dark Side of Me
A Blessed Day
Lose To Win
My Doubtful Days – Book One

My Little Talk With God
My Little Talk With God – Book Two

A Different Mood and World – Thinking

My Nagging Day
My Nagging Day – Book Two

Friday September 13, 2013

My True Love
It Would Be You
My Day

A Little Advice – Talk
1313, 2032, 2132 – The End of Man
Tata

MICHELLE'S BOOK BLOG – BOOKS 1 – 6

My Problem Day